Kids Make History

A New Look at America's Story

Susan Buckley and Elspeth Leacock

Illustrations by Randy Jones

Houghton Mifflin Company
Boston

Note to the Reader

You will notice both double and single quotation marks in this book. We use double quotation marks when we know exactly what someone said or thought. We use single quotation marks when we have invented statements based on historical evidence.

Other books by Susan Buckley and Elspeth Leacock:

Journeys for Freedom: A New Look at America's Story
Journeys in Time: A New Atlas of American History
Places in Time: A New Atlas of American History

To all the kids who are busily making tomorrow's history today
—S.B. E.L. R.J.

—and especially for Lorenzo, Lily, Conor, and Clare
—S.B.

—and Cheyenne and Willy
—E.L.

Text copyright © 2006 by Susan Washburn Buckley and Elspeth Leacock
Illustrations copyright © 2006 by Randy Jones
Book design by Kevin Ullrich

www.houghtonmifflinbooks.com

The text of this book is set in Palatino Light.
The illustrations were executed in watercolor.

Library of Congress Cataloging-in-Publication Data
Buckley, Susan Washburn.
Kids make history : a new look at America's story / Susan Buckley and Elspeth Leacock ; Illustrations by Randy Jones.
p. cm.
ISBN-13: 978-0-618-22329-9 (hardcover)
ISBN-10: 0-618-22329-0 (hardcover)
1. United States—Social life and customs—Juvenile literature. 2. Children—United States—Social life and customs—Juvenile literature. 3. United States—Social conditions—Juvenile literature. 4. Children—United States—Social conditions—Juvenile literature. 5. United States—Biography—Juvenile literature. 6. Children—United States—Biography—Juvenile literature. I. Leacock, Elspeth. II. Jones, Randy, 1950– ill. III. Title.
E161.B795 2006
973.09'9—dc22
2005036309
Printed in Singapore
TWP 10 9 8 7 6 5 4
4500217026

Introduction

KIDS MAKE HISTORY—kids like you. From the beginning, children have been part of America's story. They lived in longhouses and tepees, in brick houses and log cabins, and in the White House, too. They traveled across America as pioneers and soldiers. They worked on the Pony Express, in steel mills and ironworks, on whaling ships and canal boats, and in the cotton fields.

The twenty stories in *Kids Make History* are true stories, every one of them. Pocahontas and Samuel Collier really talked and played together at James Towne four hundred years ago. Joseph Plumb Martin did meet George Washington on the battlefield at Yorktown. Patty Reed survived with the Donner Party, crossing to California, and Laura Ingalls really lived in all of the little houses she later wrote about. Joan Zuber dashed through gunfire at Pearl Harbor, and Jukay Hsu was there when the towers fell on 9/11.

These are stories of loss and victory, bravery and celebration, building and destruction. They are part of your history, for the story of America is your story, too.

Contents

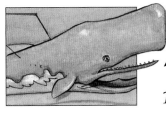

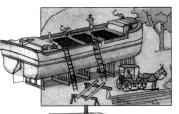

Powhatan's Favorite Daughter

1607

Pocahontas listened carefully. **1** She wanted to hear what the messengers were telling her father. Pocahontas had always been a curious girl—curious and playful. Her real name was Matoaka, but in Pocahontas's world only your family knew your real name. To everyone else in the village of Werowocomoco, she was Pocahontas, "the teasing one," the playful one. It was harder to find time to play now that she was growing up, but Pocahontas always managed. Perhaps it was because she was her father's favorite and her father was Powhatan, ruler of thousands of Algonquian people, the chief of all chiefs for a hundred miles around.

'The bearded white men are unloading their ships,' she heard the messengers say. Powhatan did not look pleased. **2** But Pocahontas had no time to find out why. Hearing her name called out, she remembered that she had work to do.

LEARNING WOMEN'S WORK

Pocahontas was not supposed to be eavesdropping at all. She was supposed to be learning all that she would need to know as a Powhatan woman: how to farm and how to cook, how to make pots and mats and baskets, even how to build houses. All through the village women were working, and girls like Pocahontas were learning. This warm May morning Pocahontas had been making baskets and carrying bags with one of her father's wives. **3** (He had *many* wives at one time.) She was proud of the bag she had completed this morning, for she had made every part of it herself. With her stepmother she had picked plants in the fields near the village. Using an oyster shell, she had scraped fiber from the stalks to make twine. Then her stepmother showed her how to weave twine into a bag for carrying food. Tomorrow, Pocahontas would take her new bag when the women went to gather food in the woods.

A WATERY WORLD

What were the bearded men doing? Pocahontas wondered. She could not see what she called their "floating islands" on the great wide river by Werowocomoco. The strangers had landed along a river just to the south. Instead, Pocahontas could see the woven fish trap where the Powhatan men and boys caught shad and herring. **6** She could see her uncles burning a tall tree into a trough shape to make a dugout canoe. She could see her aunts and cousins paddling off to gather roots for dinner. But she could see no floating islands. Pocahontas knew that there were many rivers in her father's lands, though. And she had heard stories of the great waters to the east. The bearded men had come from there, the messengers said.

COME TO STAY?

The winter snows would come before Pocahontas saw one of the bearded men. He would become her special friend. And by the next spring she would know his village well. Unlike her father, she would visit the wooden fortress that the bearded men had built. Pocahontas, the playful one, would even turn cartwheels with the boys there. **7** She knew that these newcomers were very different from anyone she had ever known before. What she did not know was that they would change her world forever.

DAWN TO DUSK

Pocahontas was busy all day long. At first light, she had bathed in the chilly water of the river nearby. When she finished making her carrying bag that day, she had a larger job: to help rebuild her house. **4** It had been a rainy spring, and the houses were leaking. Women and girls built houses with poles made from young trees that they cut in the woods. After peeling off the bark, they lashed the poles to the house frame and covered them with woven mats. **5** At the end of the day, Pocahontas would eat with her family, dipping her turtle shell into the family stew-pot. Then she would curl up inside a warm, dry house to dream.

James Towne Boy

S tanding by the burned-out fort, Sam Collier **1** smiled for the first time since the fire. Walking toward him was a young Powhatan girl. **2** Behind her, men carried baskets filled with bread and deer meat and corn. 'We are saved,' Sam cried, as his master, John Smith, **3** approached the Indians. Sam watched as the girl, Pocahontas, placed her hand over her heart in a sign of peace. Her father, Powhatan, had sent these gifts, she indicated. He knew that fire had swept through the tiny settlement days before, destroying almost everything. All but three of the buildings were now just piles of ashes. Food, clothing, supplies—almost everything was gone.

REMEMBERING

Sam knew that he was a survivor. It was hard to believe all that had happened in the thirteen months since he'd sailed from England. He remembered his excitement—off to discover a new world in Virginia, in service to the great adventurer John Smith! There were three other boys like Sam among the 105 settlers who set off in three small ships in December 1606: they were Nathaniel Peacock, James Brumfield, and Richard Mutton. Sam thought of the hard work they'd all done when they reached Virginia, chopping down trees, building the fort, planting crops. He counted off the names of those who had died from sickness that first awful summer, half of the settlers gone. And he remembered his friend and others killed in Indian attacks.

Just a week ago there were forty discouraged settlers in James Towne. Then hope arrived with Captain Newport. The captain had sailed to England to bring back more settlers. At last he had returned with eighty healthy men and supplies for the winter. Five days later, Sam heard the terrifying shout: 'Fire!'

FIRE!

No one knew how the fire started, but it probably began in the storehouse filled with food, clothing, tools—and gunpowder. As the flames leaped onto the thatched roofs, everything seemed to burn up at once. Sam and the others grabbed buckets as they ran toward the frozen river, but only the walls of the fort and three buildings could be saved. Reverend Hunt, the settlement's minister, lost all of his precious books. And, in this cold winter, all but the new settlers still living on Captain Newport's ship 4 lost every bit of clothing they weren't wearing. Were it not for the food that Powhatan sent twice a week, the settlers surely would have starved to death.

GIFTS FOR POWHATAN

Luckily, the white greyhound was on board Captain Newport's ship, 5 away from the flames. The captain had brought this rare dog as a gift for Powhatan, along with a fancy red suit and a hat. In February, John Smith and Captain Newport presented the gifts to Powhatan. "I esteem you a great Werowance," Powhatan said to Smith and Newport, making them honorary chiefs.

REBUILDING JAMES TOWNE

After the fire, Sam realized, they had to build James Towne all over again. 6 By springtime, old settlers and new would be at work. Though some wanted only to look for the gold they hoped to find in Virginia, Sam knew that building a safe settlement was the most important work he could do. That spring and again in the fall, ships arrived from England with new settlers, including two women. Sam Collier had great adventures and great hardships ahead. He would frolic with Pocahontas at the fort and he would live with her people to learn their language. 7 He would watch John Smith leave Virginia near death, and he would survive a "starving time." But for now, Sam was hard at work, building an outpost of England in America.

Evil in the Air

1692

"I am most grievously tortured!" Ann Putnam cried out. She gasped for breath, and her arms and legs twitched. As her horrified parents watched, the twelve-year-old girl tried to push away someone no one but she could see. She doubled over in agony, saying that she was being pinched and pricked "dreadfully." **1** Day after day Ann seemed to suffer from these attacks. And she was not alone. Other girls in the Puritan town of Salem had been afflicted with these mysterious and terrible fits. Their attackers were witches, they said—witches working with the Devil.

TROUBLE IN SALEM

On the farms of Salem Village **2** and the busy streets of Salem Town, **3** people were uneasy. Neighbors gossiped about one another. News of bloody Indian wars to the north spread a chill of fear. And there was an even bigger war right in Salem, the village minister warned, a war between good and evil. The Devil is all around us, he preached, and he wants "to pull it all down." The Puritan families had named their town "peace," from the Hebrew word *shalom*. But there was little peace in Salem that winter of 1692.

TORMENTED BY WITCHES

It began in January, when two girls claimed that witches were tormenting them. Soon Ann Putnam, too, cried out that she was being pinched and pricked. One by one, the girls identified three Salem women as witches who were torturing them. Then in March, Ann Putnam announced that Goodwife Martha Corey "did often appear to her and torture her." The people of Salem, already in turmoil, were shocked. Unlike the others accused, Martha Corey was a loyal member of the church. How could this be true? "You have no reason to think that I am a witch," Martha Corey said defiantly. But Ann fell down, choking and writhing on the floor when Goodwife Corey confronted her.

The next week, the judges went to Salem Village to question Martha Corey. **4** She was brought from her house **5** to the tavern. **6**

by Ann Putnam. Trying to calm down the crisis, the colony's new governor called a special court to hear the cases. On September 8, the court heard testimony against Martha Corey, and on September 10, she was found guilty of witchcraft and condemned to death. With seven others, she was hanged on Gallows Hill on September 22. **10**

As hundreds of people crowded in to hear the questioning, the courtroom was moved to the meetinghouse. **7** In front of Ann Putnam and others, the judges accused Martha Corey. **8** "Why do you hurt these persons?" they demanded. "I do not," she replied. "I am an innocent person. I never had to do with witchcraft since I was born." The judges shot out question after question, accusation after accusation, but still Martha Corey denied doing any wrong. "I cannot confess," she said. "What can I do? Many rise against me," she cried, as Ann and other girls wailed in pain and seemed to faint. **9** The courtroom became more and more hysterical, until the judges ordered Martha Corey to jail. With that, the girls' distress appeared to stop.

TO GALLOWS HILL

By May, thirty-eight people had been jailed for witchcraft, many accused

THE QUESTION

Ann went on to accuse others—fifty-three in all—but finally the accusations, the trials, and the hangings stopped. Some who had confessed as witches claimed they had been forced to make their confessions. Judges and ministers decided they had been wrong to listen to the accusations of girls like Ann Putnam. And some of the accusers had a change of heart. In 1706 a grown-up Ann Putnam asked for forgiveness for her actions. "It was a great delusion of Satan that deceived me in that sad time," she said.

What did Ann see? What did Ann believe? Even after her apology, the question hung in the air: *Why?*

Kidnapped

1743

'Come with us, boy. You seem like a lad who can win at cards,' the two men said. Peter Williamson looked up from the game he was playing on the Aberdeen wharf. Promising "amusements," the men soon persuaded the twelve-year-old boy to leave his friends and go with them. **1** They hustled Peter along the waterfront to the *Kenilworth,* **2** a ship docked in the harbor. Boys' voices and the music of a piper **3** sounded in the air. Peter looked forward to fun as he stepped below deck.

TRAPPED

In the dark cabin Peter saw boys about his age playing cards and other games. Peter thought he'd stay for a while, though he knew he'd be expected home soon. As he began to talk to the other boys, however, a terrible realization came over him. He wasn't going to be allowed to leave this boat! Little by little the story came out. Like Peter, all of the boys had been lured onto the *Kenilworth* with the promise of a good time. Once on board, they were forced to stay below deck. Sure enough, when Peter tried to leave, a sailor pushed him back into the cabin. Peter was trapped.

Meanwhile Peter's aunt—with whom he lived—was frantic. Had Peter been kidnapped? Could he have been grabbed by the men who roamed the streets and wharfs of Aberdeen, stealing young people to send to America as indentured servants? As soon as he heard the news, Peter's father walked to Aberdeen from his farm in the Scottish countryside. 'Have you seen my boy?' he asked everyone he met. Some said that Peter was being held in a barn, with other stolen boys. But Mr. Williamson could not find his son anywhere.

BOUND OVER

Unlike Peter Williamson, most indentured servants volunteered. In exchange for their trip to America, they agreed to work for a period of time—usually seven years. After that, they were free to make new lives in the colonies. More than half of the Europeans who immigrated to the colonies came as indentured servants.

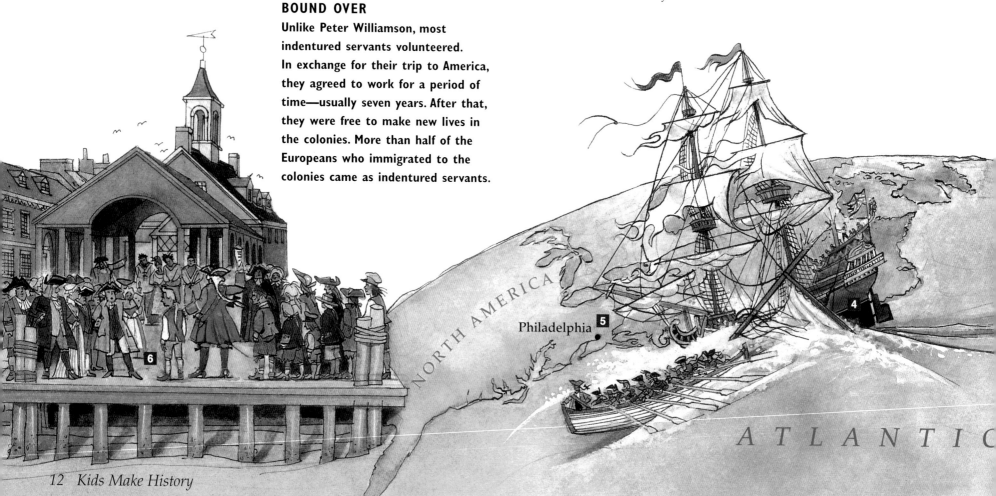

NORTH AMERICA

Philadelphia **5**

ATLANTIC

CROSSING THE ATLANTIC

Weeks passed. Every day, new boys were brought to the *Kenilworth*. As Peter's aunt had feared, they were to be sold in America as indentured servants. Finally, when about seventy boys were crowded below deck, the ship set sail. For eleven weeks the frightened, angry boys were carried across the Atlantic. With no idea when or if they would ever see their families and homes again, they could only imagine what lay ahead.

Then one night at midnight the *Kenilworth* came to a shuddering halt on a sandbar. **4** As a hard wind whipped up the waves, the ship began to tilt and take in water. Crowding the boys onto the deck, the captain and crew lowered a small boat into the water and rowed away. Peter Williamson would never forget the "cries, the shrieks, and tears" of the boys left to drown on the sinking ship.

To everyone's amazement, however, the ship did not sink. As daylight dawned, the boys could see land in the distance. And soon, a small boat arrived to take the boys to the nearby island where the captain and crew had found safety. Within days the captain had hailed a passing ship bound for Philadelphia. The boys were loaded aboard and taken to their fate in America.

SOLD LIKE SLAVES

Shortly after landing in Philadelphia, **5** Peter found himself in a large marketplace. **6** He could see women, men, and children from Africa and the Caribbean being sold as slaves. Surrounding Peter and the other stolen boys, Americans urgently bid on them, purchasing their services

for a seven-year indenture—seven years of servitude for sixteen pounds. A man with a kind face bought Peter Williamson and led him away from the market. Peter never saw any of the other boys again.

A KIND MAN

Peter was lucky. Hugh Wilson, who owned Peter's life for the next seven years, had been a stolen boy himself. He knew what it felt like to be kidnapped, so he was a gentle master. At first he gave the boy only small jobs to do. Seeing people around him reading and writing, Peter decided that he wanted to go to school in his spare time. 'If you let me go to school,' he told Hugh Wilson, 'I will serve a year longer than the contract by which I was bound.' Wilson agreed, and for the next five years Peter went to school.

When Peter was seventeen years old, Hugh Wilson died. As a reward for faithful service, the kind man left Peter £200, a good horse, a saddle, and all of his clothing. "Being now my own master, having money in my pocket, and all other necessaries," Peter Williamson wrote, he was a free man at last.

DANGEROUS STREETS

For about six years in the 1740s, children were kidnapped every day on the streets of Aberdeen, Scotland. Local officials and merchants took part in the evil, making money by selling the lives of others. Sometimes they even persuaded poor parents to sell their children into servitude.

GREENLAND

ICELAND

OCEAN

GREAT BRITAIN

Aberdeen

EUROPE

Yankee Doodle Soldier

Battle of Monmouth

1776

One July evening in 1776, Joseph Plumb Martin dipped a pen in ink and signed up to be a soldier in the Continental Army. **1** The fifteen-year-old Connecticut boy knew that he was "as warm a patriot as the best of them." Sad and worried, Joseph's family prepared to send him off to war. They packed his knapsack with clothing, cake, cheese, and a small Bible. "I was now what I had long wished to be, a soldier," Joseph said. "I had obtained my heart's desire; it was now my business to prove myself equal to my profession."

THE FIRST BATTLE

"Like a shower of hail," the British cannon fire poured over the soldiers. It was August 1776, and this was Joseph Martin's first battle. Under the command of General George Washington, the Americans were defending New York City against the British. After crossing to Long Island by ferry, Joseph's regiment had met the enemy in a cornfield. **2** By nighttime, the American officers knew their troops were outnumbered. They whispered orders to their soldiers. Not a word, not a cough, was permitted as Joseph and the other soldiers retreated across the river to safety in New York City. Joseph had imagined "the horrors of battle . . . in all their hideousness" but had vowed to do his duty as well as he could—and he had.

"FATIGUE, HUNGER, AND COLD"

Fight and retreat, fight and retreat **3**—for all the next year, Joseph Martin endured the hardships of soldiering. Always with him, he said, were his "constant companions, Fatigue, Hunger, and Cold." To pass the winter cold, soldiers rested in winter camps. But those at Valley Forge **4** were in such "truly forlorn condition" that Joseph thought they would not survive.

When winter was over, though, General Washington led his troops out to chase the British army. At the end of June, at Monmouth Court House in New Jersey, **5** Joseph fought fiercely and well. With cannonballs crashing around him, Joseph saw a woman helping her husband fight. As he watched, a cannonball ripped right through Molly Pitcher's petticoats and passed out the other side. The next day the cannons were silent, and Joseph Martin and his regiment marched away. Neither side had won a real victory.

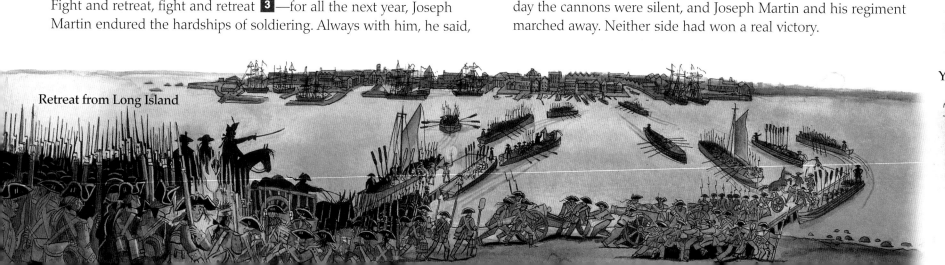

Retreat from Long Island

MARYLAND

Yorktown

VIRGINIA

6

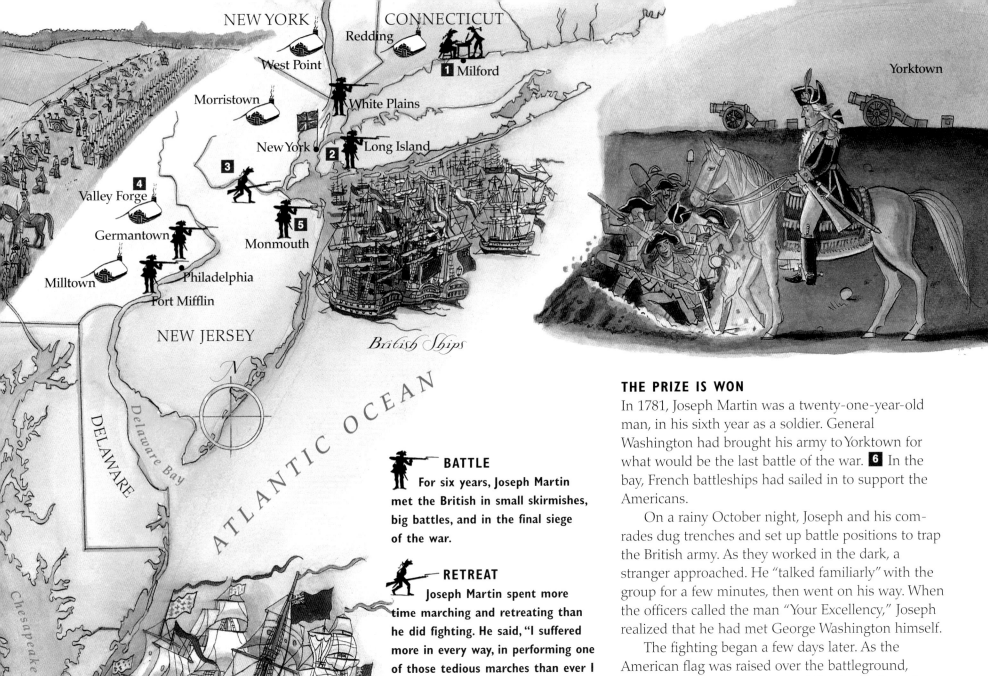

NEW YORK CONNECTICUT

Redding

West Point

1 Milford

Morristown

White Plains

New York **2** Long Island

3

4

Valley Forge

Germantown

5

Monmouth

Milltown

Philadelphia

Fort Mifflin

NEW JERSEY

British Ships

DELAWARE

Delaware Bay

ATLANTIC OCEAN

Chesapeake Bay

British Ships

French Ships

Yorktown

BATTLE
For six years, Joseph Martin met the British in small skirmishes, big battles, and in the final siege of the war.

RETREAT
Joseph Martin spent more time marching and retreating than he did fighting. He said, "I suffered more in every way, in performing one of those tedious marches than ever I did in fighting the hottest battle."

WINTER CAMP
When it was too cold to fight, the soldiers huddled together in winter camps. If they didn't freeze first, Joseph feared, they would starve to death.

THE PRIZE IS WON

In 1781, Joseph Martin was a twenty-one-year-old man, in his sixth year as a soldier. General Washington had brought his army to Yorktown for what would be the last battle of the war. **6** In the bay, French battleships had sailed in to support the Americans.

On a rainy October night, Joseph and his comrades dug trenches and set up battle positions to trap the British army. As they worked in the dark, a stranger approached. He "talked familiarly" with the group for a few minutes, then went on his way. When the officers called the man "Your Excellency," Joseph realized that he had met George Washington himself.

The fighting began a few days later. As the American flag was raised over the battleground, Joseph felt "a secret pride" swell his heart. Soon he found himself in the heart of the battle as "shells with their fiery trains" flew through the air. For days, Joseph fought for twenty-four hours at a stretch. At last, on October 17, the British surrendered. "The war was over, the prize won," Joseph would later write. It was a victory thousands had died for, the prize of a free nation.

The House on the Hill

1838

John Rankin Jr. snuggled deeper into the warmth of his bed. **1** He'd been dreaming, remembering the thrill of flying across the frozen Ohio River, which lay below his hilltop house. Just a few days before, the twelve-year-old boy had been skating on the river with half the men and boys who lived in Ripley, Ohio. But no one had ventured onto the river since a loud crack was heard when one young man dared to drive his horse and sleigh right out onto the ice.

ACROSS THE RIVER

Directly across the river from the Rankin house, a young woman hesitated at the edge of the Ohio. **2** Standing in the dark, snowy woods, Eliza clutched her two-year-old child in one arm and held a long fence rail in the other. Across the river lay hope for freedom from a life of slavery—if only she could reach the other side. Eliza knew that crossing the river now could be deadly, for the ice was breaking up along the banks. She also knew that she could never go back—to the farm in Kentucky, to the master who was planning to sell her child, to the cruel life of slavery. In Ohio, slavery was outlawed, but escaping slaves like Eliza could be captured and returned. Eliza knew that she

TO THE LIGHT OF HOPE

That night, Chancey Shaw did something that he had never done before: he led an escaping slave to safety. Shaw could not bring himself to send this brave woman and her child back to slavery. Instead, he took Eliza into Ripley and pointed up the hill to the house that she had heard of, **6** the house where there was always a lantern in the window, promising help to those who needed it. **7** 'Climb the stairs. The door will be open, and the Rankin family will help you,' Shaw said.

IN THE HOUSE ON THE HILL

In the house on the hill, John Rankin Jr. was still dreaming when he heard his father call softly. 'John, Calvin, come downstairs *now*.' John nudged his older brother, and both boys dressed quickly and warmly. They knew what was waiting for them downstairs—someone fleeing slavery. It had been the same for years: in the dark of night, men, women, families, had crossed the river and climbed the stairs to the house on the hill. And Reverend John Rankin and his family had hidden them, then guided them on to the next stop on their way to Canada.

When John Jr. and Calvin rushed downstairs, **8** they saw Eliza and her child wrapped in blankets, shivering by the fire as Mrs. Rankin found dry clothes for them. **9** "She's crossed the river on the ice!" Reverend Rankin told the boys in amazement. They looked at Eliza in disbelief. How could anyone have been brave enough to do that now that the ice was breaking?

was not yet safe, but in Ohio she could begin the journey to Canada and freedom. And she knew that there was a family across this river who would help her.

Suddenly Eliza heard a dreaded sound—slave catchers were calling to their barking dogs, coming to capture her. **3** She could wait no longer. Using the fence rail for balance, Eliza stepped out onto the river. Instantly she felt herself sinking into frigid water as the ice crumbled beneath her. Struggling onto firm ice, Eliza moved out onto the wide river. Three times the surface gave way under her feet, plunging her into peril. Each time the desperate woman thrust her child ahead onto solid ice as she climbed out of the water. **4** Finally, exhausted and freezing, Eliza and the child reached the solid ground of safety, or so she prayed. Then Chancey Shaw stepped out of the shadows. **5** At once, Eliza knew that the man was a slave catcher, but she did not have the strength to flee.

ON THE WAY

'You'll need to leave right away to take them to Reverend Gilliland's house and be back before daybreak,' Reverend Rankin told the boys. As soon as Eliza and the child were warm enough, they set out across the snowy hills. **10** John walked behind with Eliza while Calvin carried the child. Staying in the shadows as much as they could, the boys and Eliza watched for slave catchers. None saw them, and before dawn Eliza and her child were in the safe hands of Reverend Gilliland. As John Jr. wished her well, he wondered how many places she would have to hide before she reached safety. And he wondered who would seek refuge in the house on the hill tomorrow.

"Never Take No Cutoffs"

1846

California! It seemed like such a good idea. As spring arrived in Illinois, twelve-year-old Virginia Reed was ready for adventure. All winter long her stepfather, James Reed, and his friends George and Jacob Donner had pored over a new book, *The Emigrants' Guide to Oregon and California* by Lansford W. Hastings. Hastings told of California's sunshine and cheap, fertile land. The four-month trip wouldn't be difficult, Hastings promised. He even knew of a shortcut that might save time. Friends thought they were insane to take what must be a dangerous journey. But the Reeds and the Donners didn't listen. They were ready for California.

SETTING OUT

By late April the Reeds and the Donners left home **1** in nine covered wagons, three for each family. Although most of the thirty-four travelers walked beside the tightly packed wagons, Virginia rode next to her stepfather on her beloved horse, Billy. James Reed had made one of his wagons larger than the others—as big as a palace, some said—for the comfort of his wife's ailing mother, Sarah Keyes. Virginia's little sister, Patty, stayed inside the big wagon with her grandmother, pulling aside the canvas cover so that the old woman could wave goodbye.

CROSSING THE PLAINS

Past Independence, Missouri, **2** the wagons headed west with other wagon parties. Within weeks, Sarah Keyes was dead, buried along the trail near the Big Blue River. **3** "We miss her very much," Virginia wrote to her cousins. So much was happening, though, that she soon called the journey "an ideal pleasure trip." She galloped across the plain amid herds of buffalo near Chimney Rock **4** and celebrated the Fourth of July. By mid-July, the wagons had traveled more than a thousand miles across the continent to Independence Rock.

THINGS GO WRONG

Having crossed the Rocky Mountains, the travelers reached the moment of decision: whether to take the proven route or the cutoff Hastings recommended. The Donner party voted to take the Hastings cutoff, a choice that led them into a nightmare. **5** Crossing the Wasatch Mountains, **6** they cut through trees and brush so thick they traveled only thirty miles in eighteen days. On the Great Salt Lake Desert, after two days without water, Virginia said, "It seemed as though the hand of death had been laid upon the country." **7** Then one day, when tempers flared, James Reed stabbed and killed a man. As his horrified family watched, **8** the Donner party sent Reed off alone on horseback, with only the gun and the food that Virginia could sneak to him.

DISASTER AT TRUCKEE LAKE

Straggling into the Sierra Nevada mountains in late October, **9** the Donner party were only sixty miles from safety on the other side. But early snowstorms trapped them at Truckee Lake, high in the mountains. **10** Before help could arrive, four months would pass — four months of starvation, misery, and death. Some tried to escape on snowshoes, but most had to turn back. By January the Reeds had only the skin of dead oxen to boil and eat. They even ate the leather covers off their books.

On the other side of the mountains, rescue parties tried and failed to reach the dying travelers. Among the rescuers was James Reed, who had found his way to safety months earlier. On February 27, Virginia Reed looked across the snow and saw her stepfather, come to save them. **11** "Thank God we have . . . got through," Virginia later wrote to a cousin. But she warned, "Never take no cutoffs."

Independence Rock

JOHN REED

Chimney Rock

5 Fort Laramie

4

MISSOURI

1 Springfield

ILLINOIS

Mississippi River

2 Independence

3

UNORGANIZED TERRITORY

Pony Rider

1854

Nick Wilson was twelve years old, but he felt as though he had been herding sheep for a hundred years. The Wilsons had come west in a covered wagon four years earlier, settling just south of the Great Salt Lake in Utah. Nick was lonely and bored out on the range, taking care of the animals by himself. **1** The boy was looking for adventure, and he was about to find it.

WHITE INDIAN BOY

One day in August, a group of Shoshone Indian men camped near Nick and his sheep. When a Shoshone led over a little pinto pony, Nick could not take his eyes off the horse. 'You can keep the pony if you come away with us,' the Shoshone said. "I would rather have that pony than anything else I ever saw," Nick answered. And with that, Nick Wilson left home—without a word to his family. **2**

At the Shoshone camp, a tall man and an old woman were waiting. **3** 'I, Washakie the chief, am your new brother,' the man told him. 'And this is our mother.' The Indian woman cried as she put her hand on Nick's head. Her other sons had died, and Nick was to be her new child.

Soon they set out for the great tribal meeting that the Shoshone chiefs held every three years. **4** Along the way they hunted buffalo, **5** and Washakie got five hundred pounds of meat for the family. When they reached Deer Lodge Valley, about six thousand Shoshone were camped in tepees all along a stream. **6**

For the next two years, Nick Wilson traveled with his Indian family as they hunted the buffalo herds and fought their enemies. He learned the Shoshone ways.

WASHINGTON TERRITORY

UTAH TERRITORY

Great Salt Lake

Salt Lake Cit

Oregon Trail

Pony Express

Sacramento

CALIFORNIA

N

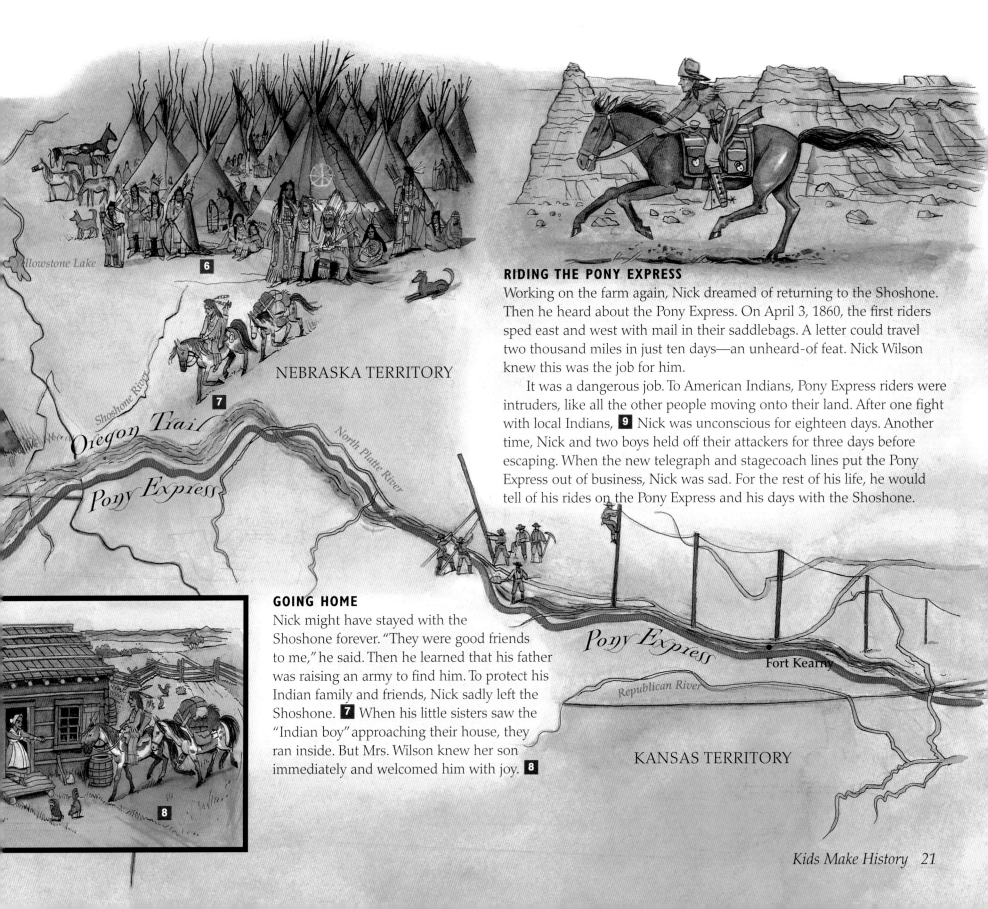

RIDING THE PONY EXPRESS

Working on the farm again, Nick dreamed of returning to the Shoshone. Then he heard about the Pony Express. On April 3, 1860, the first riders sped east and west with mail in their saddlebags. A letter could travel two thousand miles in just ten days—an unheard-of feat. Nick Wilson knew this was the job for him.

It was a dangerous job. To American Indians, Pony Express riders were intruders, like all the other people moving onto their land. After one fight with local Indians, **9** Nick was unconscious for eighteen days. Another time, Nick and two boys held off their attackers for three days before escaping. When the new telegraph and stagecoach lines put the Pony Express out of business, Nick was sad. For the rest of his life, he would tell of his rides on the Pony Express and his days with the Shoshone.

NEBRASKA TERRITORY

GOING HOME

Nick might have stayed with the Shoshone forever. "They were good friends to me," he said. Then he learned that his father was raising an army to find him. To protect his Indian family and friends, Nick sadly left the Shoshone. **7** When his little sisters saw the "Indian boy" approaching their house, they ran inside. But Mrs. Wilson knew her son immediately and welcomed him with joy. **8**

KANSAS TERRITORY

Fort Kearny

Republican River

Pony Express

Oregon Trail

Shoshone River

North Platte River

Yellowstone Lake

Pull-Up Boy

1860

"Up!" his father shouted, and Marty Myers pulled up the heavy furnace door. Marty forced himself not to yank back from the blast of heat that shot out of the furnace. Quickly, Martin Myers Sr. thrust an iron rod into the white-hot sea of melted metal and began to stir. Sweat poured down the blackened faces of father and son. Marty knew that he was only part of the way through his ten-hour workday, but he was determined not to slow down. Marty was six years old, a brand-new worker at the Sligo Iron Works. **1**

It had been dark when he left home with his father that morning, but Marty didn't mind. He was proud to be going to work, proud to be learning a trade at his father's side. His dad, Martin Myers, had come all the way from Germany to work in the iron industry that was turning Pittsburgh into the greatest manufacturing city in the United States. Margaret and Mary, Marty's sisters, were going to school. His two little brothers were too young to work, but Marty was just the age to start.

WORKING IRON

All day at the ironworks, Marty worked with his father as a pull-up boy. **2** It was his job to pull up the iron door of the puddling furnace **3** so that Martin Myers **4** could melt, clear, boil, ball, and draw out the five hundred pounds of pig iron that it contained. Marty knew that his father's job as a puddler was one of the most important at the ironworks, and it was the job that he was preparing to do one day. So he watched carefully as his father worked the iron.

When the coal fire was hot enough—almost 3500 degrees—Marty held the door open just long enough for the pig iron to be shoveled into the furnace. After about twenty minutes, Martin Myers called out to his son to pull up the door again. With an iron rod

IN THE NEIGHBORHOOD
Surrounding the factories were the neighborhoods where workers lived. In the churches, **7** schools, **8** stores, and homes, life revolved around the schedules and the wages and work of the iron mills.

called a rabble, **5** Martin began to stir the hot melted iron until he had cleared it of impurities. Marty stared in wonder at the muscles in his father's arms as Martin stirred the 125-pound rabble through the melted iron for ten minutes until it began to boil. With the heat pouring over them, Martin stirred and Marty watched, trying to memorize every move his father made. As the "iron soup" became thicker and thicker, Martin Myers began to work it into three balls. Putting his rabble aside, he used giant tongs to draw the three massive balls of iron out of the furnace. Then, as other workers took the balls away, Martin and Marty got ready to begin the process all over again.

A MOUNTAIN OF COAL

Ironworks like the Sligo depended on iron ore, limestone, and coal. The hills of Pittsburgh were filled with coal, mined to heat the iron-works' furnaces. Iron ore came from the north by the trainload. **9** Barges brought the limestone from nearby quarries. **10**

CITY OF SMOKE

More than 150 furnaces processed so much iron in Pittsburgh that the sky was always dark with coal dust. **11** Flames lit up the blackness so that the city looked like "hell with the lid off," one visitor said.

AT HOME

At 6 Carson Street, **12** in a house provided by the Sligo, Mrs. Myers was busy. With a family of six to care for, she was hard at work all day long.

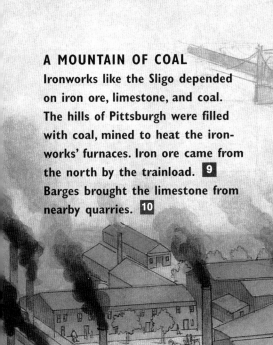

SWEAT, SOOT, AND DREAMS

Sweat covered Marty's face and arms. Black with soot from the coal fire, Marty wiped his eyes clear with his cap. Then he began to help his father shovel the coal **6** that kept the furnace flaming like a "fiery lake."

Finally, Marty's long day was almost over. Tomorrow would be Sunday, the only day of the week when the boy did not work. On Sundays, the Myers family had a big dinner after church. As Marty began to daydream about his mother's delicious pies, he heard his father shout. "Up!" Martin Myers called out, and Marty pulled up the door one more time.

Working for Freedom

1863

Susie Baker listened proudly as the words of freedom were read aloud. Anyone held as a slave in the states "in rebellion against the United States, shall be then, thenceforward, and forever free," President Lincoln had written. It was January 1, 1863, and the First South Carolina Volunteers were celebrating the Emancipation Proclamation. Flags waved, ministers spoke, soldiers sang and shouted "Hurrah!" throughout the camp. The army cooks roasted whole oxen for a barbecue. "It was a glorious day for us all," Susie wrote.

When the day was over and taps sounded through the camp, fourteen-year-old Susie thought back over her path to that day. She remembered her childhood in slavery. She remembered learning to read and write even though it was forbidden for slaves to do so. She thought of the beginning of the Civil War and of the time, just months before, when she was freed from slavery by a Northern general. Susie Baker knew what it felt like to be enslaved and to be free. She knew what was at the heart of this war.

ESCAPE TO FREEDOM

When Susie was thirteen, Union soldiers had captured the Confederate fort **1** guarding her hometown of Savannah, Georgia. After the guns were silenced, the Union general declared all slaves in the area free. With that, Susie's uncle left the city with his family and Susie. **2** He knew that they would be safer on the coastal islands now held by Union soldiers. From St. Catherine Island they were taken by gunboat **3** to St. Simon's Island. It was there, to her "unbounded joy," that Susie saw her first "Yankee." And it was there that Susie became a teacher. The commander of the Union soldiers asked her to teach the island children—and some adults—"all of them so eager to learn to read, to read above anything else." **4** It was there too that the first regiment of black soldiers was formed, the First South Carolina Volunteers. Soon Susie was both laundering the soldiers' clothes and teaching them to read.

GEORGIA

St. Simon's Island

St. Catherine Island

Satilla River

Gun Boat

Jacksonville

FLORIDA

ATLANTIC OCEAN

CAMP LIFE

As fighting advanced toward the islands, the regiment was moved to Camp Saxton, near Beaufort, South Carolina, and Susie went along. Soon afterward smallpox broke out in the camp and Susie took on a new job—nursing the soldiers struck by the deadly disease. **5** When the regiment was ordered to Jacksonville, Florida, **6** Susie and several other young women went along as nurses. Fighting was so fierce that Susie "expected every moment to be killed by a shell." After a few weeks, the regiment returned to Camp Saxton and then moved to a new site. **7** They named it Camp Shaw, to honor Colonel Robert Gould Shaw, the brave leader of the Massachusetts Fifty-fourth, another black regiment. Sometimes the enemy soldiers were so close that Susie could hear them talking. She learned to handle a gun and "shoot straight."

The fighting continued. Sometimes Susie went to Fort Wagner **8** "to watch the gunners send their shells into Charleston." By the next year the regiment was moving from one island camp to another. Then they were ordered to attack Fort Gregg. Susie helped "her boys" pack their knapsacks, and she nursed them when they returned with "wounds of all kinds imaginable."

WAR'S END

By 1865 the war was crashing to a close. Susie went into Charleston **9** with the regiment as Southern troops fled a burning city. "It was a terrible scene," she remembered, with women and children left behind "to suffer and perish in the flames." There and in Savannah, Susie cared for the sick and the wounded. Susie stayed with "her boys" until 1866, when the regiment was dismissed. "The hour is at hand when we must separate forever," their commander declared, "and nothing can take from us the pride we feel when we look upon the history of the First South Carolina Volunteers, the first black regiment that ever bore arms in defense of freedom on the continent of America." It was a proud day for the soldiers and for the girl who had worked for freedom with them.

Charleston

Fort Pinckney

9

Fort Johnson

Fort Sumpter

Fort Gregg

Fort Wagner

Fort Moultrie

8

Fort Wagner

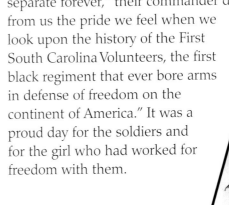

Savannah River

2

Savannah •

Union Troops

1

Fort Pulaski

Camp Shaw •

• Camp Saxton

7

5

SOUTH CAROLINA

N

Fort Pulaski

Gun Boat

• Charleston

Pioneer Girl

1868

Little Laura Ingalls was on her way west. The two covered wagons were packed full. Laura's Ma and Pa and her sister, Mary, were in one wagon, **1** her aunt, uncle, and cousins in the other. Jack, the bulldog, trotted around, ready to go. Out in front of Grandpa's house in the Big Woods, the rest of the family waved goodbye. Just over a year ago, Laura had been born in a little house in those Big Woods. Her father loved the woods, but he loved open spaces even more. 'It's getting too crowded here,' Pa had said. So one May day, the Ingalls family set out to try their luck on the prairie.

THE LITTLE HOUSE ON THE PRAIRIE

They crossed rivers **2** and miles of grasslands. Thousands of pioneers like the Ingalls family were claiming land in Kansas, land that really belonged to the Osage Indians. The railroad companies said they would buy the land, then sell it cheap to the new settlers. So Pa and Ma settled the family near the new town of Independence. Haytown, the Osage called it, for the settlers were putting up buildings with roofs of hay.

Down by the creek, Pa found enough trees to cut for logs. It took about fifty of them to build the Ingallses' little house on the prairie. **3** But after a year, unsure that they could ever get the right to buy their land from the Osage, Pa and Ma decided to return to the Big Woods. They harnessed the horses Pet and Patty to the wagons and turned them back toward the Big Woods. **4**

ON THE BANKS OF PLUM CREEK

After a few years, Pa was itching to move west again. 'The railroad is opening land in Minnesota,' he said. 'When the river is frozen hard enough for us to cross, we'll head out again.' Just before Laura's seventh

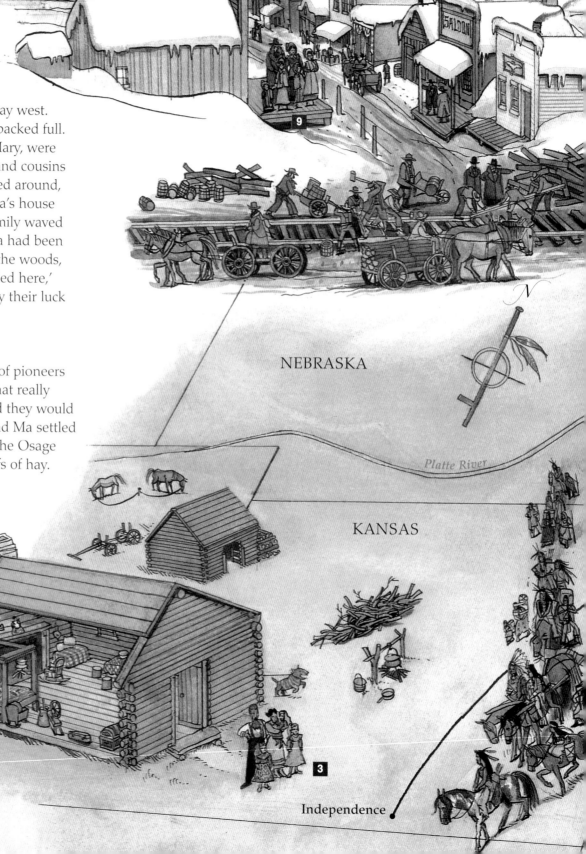

NEBRASKA

Platte River

KANSAS

Independence

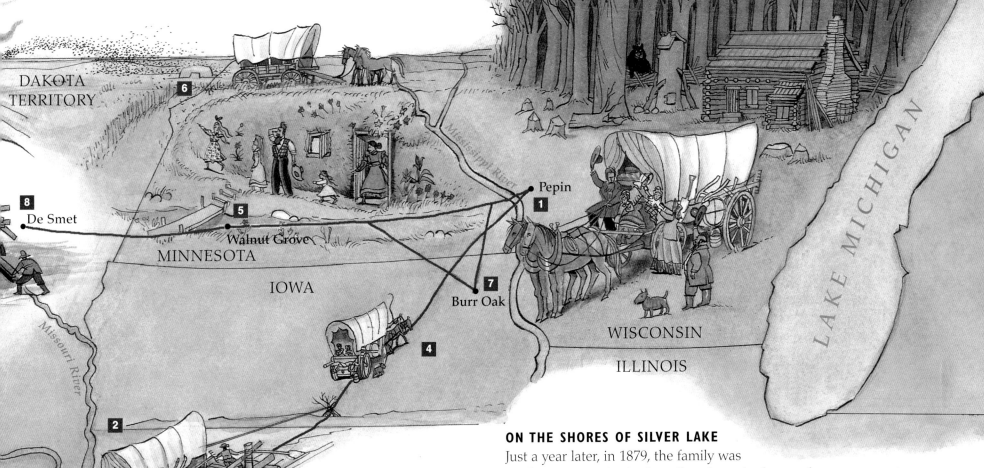

DAKOTA TERRITORY

6

MINNESOTA

5
Walnut Grove

8
De Smet

Pepin
1

IOWA

7
Burr Oak

4

2

Mississippi River

Missouri River

WISCONSIN

ILLINOIS

LAKE MICHIGAN

birthday, in February, the family packed up the wagon and went west. This time Pa was able to buy land—172 acres near the town of Walnut Grove. Laura could hardly believe her eyes when she saw their first house, a sod dugout on the banks of Plum Creek. **5** Laura loved the odd house. What she did not love were the grasshoppers. They came in the springtime, in a horde so thick it darkened the sky. Pa's first wheat crop was just coming up, and they ate every plant and stalk in sight. **6**

When the same thing happened the next spring, the Ingallses had had enough. With another family, they left Minnesota and went to Iowa. **7** Pa tried different jobs in a little town there, but somehow nothing worked out. Like Pa, Laura longed for the great open skies of the prairie, and after a year, the Ingalls family returned to Walnut Grove.

ON THE SHORES OF SILVER LAKE

Just a year later, in 1879, the family was on the move again. As the railroads pushed west, the government was selling cheap land in the Dakota Territory. Crews of two hundred men were laying track across the broad grasslands, starting new towns such as De Smet **8** every eight to twelve miles along the way. The Ingallses settled along the shores of Silver Lake. This must be their last move, Ma said, and Laura was glad.

Once again Pa built a little house, but when winter came he moved the family into town. **9** The snows began in October that year and lasted for six months. When spring blossomed at last, the family went back to the farm. Pa plowed fields and planted crops. Ma and the girls—there were four now—planted a garden and cared for the cows and chickens and pigs.

Laura was growing up, and she wanted to help even more. At fifteen, before her own schooling was even finished, Laura became a teacher herself. And a few years later, a young homesteader named Almanzo Wilder asked her to marry him. Laura's childhood was over. But in the years to come, she would remember all of the little houses and would share their stories with the world.

"There Blows!"

1875

It was pitch dark and smelly in the bottom of the whaling ship *Union*. George Fred Tilton felt his way toward the very front of the ship, looking for a hiding place. When he found a dry spot, he settled in for the night, but he was too scared to sleep. George Fred had been trying to get onto a whaling ship for weeks. In fact, he'd been dreaming of it for as long as he could remember. Back home on Martha's Vineyard, he'd listened to the tales of the whalers, men who had sailed around the world hunting the giant creatures of the sea. But George Fred was only fourteen years old, and when he asked his parents if he could go to sea, they said no. The boy was determined, though. When he heard that the *Union* would be shipping out of New Bedford **1** in June, he sneaked away from home, and now here he was, stowed away on a whaling ship, **2** praying that he wouldn't be caught before it sailed.

OUT TO SEA

On the morning of June 8, when the full sails were up and the ship's bow began to cut through the choppy sea, George Fred was afraid "the water would burst right through." But he stayed hidden for two days just to be sure the captain wouldn't take him back to shore. When the boy finally came up on deck, the captain was amazed. "Do you know where you are going?" he demanded. "Why, whaling, I suppose," George Fred replied. It was too late to turn back, so the captain put the stowaway to work. Now that he wasn't scared anymore, George Fred got seasick. 'You're just a "greenie,"' the rest of the crew said. Like most new whalers, the boy threw up until he almost turned green!

RAISING A WHALE

As the *Union* sailed southeast toward the whaling grounds, George Fred "learned the ropes"—which ropes moved which sails and how to climb high in the rigging, the network of ropes that controls the sails. At the

end of June, the ship reached Bermuda. Two weeks later, George Fred heard the cry "There blows!" A giant sperm whale rose out of the water nearby, spouting water from its blow hole. "I was the most excited and anxious boy in the world," George Fred remembered. "I don't suppose that anyone ever moved any faster than I did when we got the order to lower."

In a flash, the crew lowered and boarded the small boats they used to chase the whale. **3** As they raced toward the great animal, George Fred rowed harder than he ever thought he could. Every time the whale dove and came up, it seemed as though a hurricane was exploding out of the ocean. When they were almost on top of the whale, the harpooner

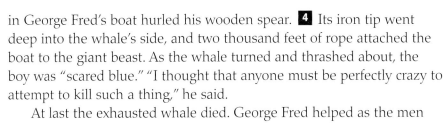

in George Fred's boat hurled his wooden spear. **4** Its iron tip went deep into the whale's side, and two thousand feet of rope attached the boat to the giant beast. As the whale turned and thrashed about, the boy was "scared blue." "I thought that anyone must be perfectly crazy to attempt to kill such a thing," he said.

At last the exhausted whale died. George Fred helped as the men tied the animal to the side of the ship and then began the "cutting in." Working quickly, the crew cut off about a ton of the whale's flesh—the fatty layer called blubber—and raised it to the ship. On the ship's deck, they melted chunks of blubber into oil in huge kettles set in a brick furnace called the tryworks. **5** George Fred's first whale made fifty barrels of the valuable oil.

SAILING THE ATLANTIC

For the next thirteen months, George Fred sailed the Atlantic on the *Union*—to the Azores, **6** to the Cape Verde Islands, **7** and back. The crew "raised"—sighted —other whales and captured some of them, but none was as large as George Fred's first whale. In September 1876, the *Union* docked in New Bedford again. When George Fred made his way home, he was a year older and sixty-five pounds heavier. "I was richer in experience and darned little else," he said, for he owed more than his pay for the clothes and supplies he'd bought. Still, he was ready to go back. "I had been across the ocean and at sea for over a year, had seen whales killed and returned to tell the tale. What more could a boy want?" he said.

36/36
Grounds

EUROPE

Azores

Steen

AFRICA

6

7 Cape Verde
Islands

"A Most Wonderful Sight"

1893

"Dear Mamma, Tomorrow we are going to start with vigor," Jane Sever wrote. It was July 21, and sixteen-year-old Jane had just arrived from Massachusetts to visit the great Chicago world's fair, the World's Columbian Exposition. Since the fair had opened in May, Jane—like thousands around the country—had dreamed of seeing its wonders.

The next day Jane set out for the fair with Miss Mabel, a family friend. They began their visit at the Midway Plaisance, almost a mile of "shows and sights"—from a balloon ride 1,500 feet into the air to the Sliding Railroad that traveled a hundred miles an hour! The wonderful Ferris wheel was there too. **1** Towering above the fairgrounds, it had been the first thing they saw as they arrived in Chicago. But Jane and Miss Mabel decided to save that thrill for later. They spent much of the day in the Anthropological Building, where Jane bought a tiny basket from one of the many American Indians who were themselves on display. Best of all were the fireworks that night. "It was a most wonderful sight," Jane wrote. They lit up Jane's favorite spot at the fair: the Peristyle, designed to look like a Greek temple. **2**

On another day, Jane and Miss Mabel **3** stood at one end of the Grand Basin. **4** They gazed at the golden Statue of the Republic, **5** sixty-five feet tall, the largest sculpture ever made in America. It stood in front of the Peristyle. Boats—even Venetian gondolas **6**—sailed across the basin. Ahead on one side of the basin was the fair's largest structure, the Manufactures Building **7**—made with six thousand tons of steel—where the products of industry were proudly displayed. Across the basin Jane could see the statue of the goddess Diana on top of the Agriculture Building. **8** That night there was "a most wonderful sight" as the electric fountains **9** shimmered with lights. "It seemed as if one must be in Fairyland," Jane wrote. All in all, Jane thought, "you could never imagine anything so beautiful" as the World's Columbian Exposition.

HONORING COLUMBUS

To celebrate the four hundredth anniversary of the arrival of Columbus in the Americas, the country wanted to show off "the wonderful achievements of the new age . . . as the most effective means of increasing the fraternity, progress, prosperity, and peace of mankind."

A BIG SUCCESS

Everything about the fair was big: $26 million and two years to construct the buildings; 64 million gallons of water consumed every day; 120 railroad cars filled with glass for windows; more than 700,000 visitors on the biggest day of the fair; and on and on. Over the six months that the fair was open, more than 7 million people came to see the sights.

MR. FERRIS'S INVENTION

The engineer George Ferris built the world's first Ferris wheel for the fair. The gigantic steel wheel towered more than 250 feet in the air— higher than a twenty-story building. Each of its thirty-six cars was the size of a bus, holding sixty passengers. More than 2,100 people could take the twenty-minute roundtrip ride at a time.

High Jinks in the White House

1902

The president of the United States roared with laughter. **1** It was just before Christmas, and Theodore Roosevelt's six children were turning the White House into a playground. Alice—at eighteen, the oldest—had just announced that she had had enough of this silliness. As her father shook his head and laughed, Alice waltzed down the hallway with Emily Spinach, her bright green snake, wrapped around her arm. **2**

Ethel and Kermit were having a race. **3** Ethel always wanted to win, but now she was so happy to see her favorite brother, Kermit, that she didn't care. Kermit was thirteen, in his first year away at boarding school. Boarding school was nothing like being home, Kermit thought, nothing like the high jinks in the White House. He could hear the squeals of his little brothers Archie and Quentin as they slid down the front stairs on tin trays. **4** Rushing upstairs, messenger Arthur Simmons stepped out of the way. 'Those boys!' he said, shaking his head. **5**

Meanwhile, Ted, the oldest Roosevelt boy, was planning a surprise. Like Kermit, Ted was happy to be home from school. At school he didn't have a pony—and even if he had had one, he certainly couldn't have taken it up and down in the elevator! **6** Ted knew that his mother was expecting friends that afternoon. He thought he might surprise them with a visit from Algonquin, the family's calico pony.

Nothing her children did would surprise Edith Roosevelt, however. Calmly and happily, she made plans with White House steward Henry Pinkney. 'Those children are just cutting loose,' she heard electrician Ike Hoover say. **7** Mrs. Roosevelt smiled and agreed.

AT HOME UPSTAIRS

This would be the Roosevelts' second Christmas at the White House, but this year everything was different. The family was just settling in to a newly redecorated home. The special public rooms were on the first floor, but the second floor was where the family lived (and where most of the high jinks took place). Mrs. Roosevelt's sitting room **8** was everyone's favorite spot.

THE LADIES' CABINET

Edith Roosevelt was a very busy first lady. With her very busy husband and six very busy children swirling around her, Mrs. Roosevelt entertained hundreds of people every week. She also held meetings in the library **9** with the wives of cabinet members. (All of the advisers in the president's cabinet were men in those days.) Now, however, the library was the place where Christmas packages were hidden from the children's eyes!

DEVOURING BOOKS

In his private study, **10** Theodore Roosevelt surrounded himself with books. In fact, he and his children read so much that people said they "devoured books"—when they weren't playing, that is.

Low Bridge!

1909

Richard Garrity poked his older brother James. 'We can leave soon,' he said excitedly. Richard, James, and their little sister, Margaret, stood on top of the canal boat's cabin. **1** Everywhere they looked, someone or something was moving. Hired men were unloading the last of the cargo of lumber onto the shore. **2** Monkey Joe, the driver, was guiding mules down the ramp, ready to hook them up to the tow ropes. **3** Mr. Garrity was walking up and down, calling out orders to keep everything going. **4** And the smells and sounds coming from the cabin told the children that their mother was cooking lunch and that baby Charlie was hungry. **5**

The Garritys and their canal boat, the *Sol Goldsmith*, had been in Syracuse, New York, **6** for almost a week—twice as long as it had taken them to travel down the Erie Canal from Tonawanda. For the six-month canal season, from mid-May to mid-November, Mr. Garrity worked the canal with his boat, his driver, his mules, and his family.

STOCKING UP

Sure enough, that evening the *Sol Goldsmith* turned west toward home. "Hooraw," Monkey Joe called out as the three-mule team slowly towed the boat away from the city. Twelve hours later, *Sol Goldsmith* had traveled the thirty miles to Port Byron. **7** At the canal store Mr. Garrity bought some new collars, towlines, and oats for the mules, and Mrs. Garrity stocked up on food for the trip home. The children just waited and smiled, for at the end the storeowner always gave them a present: a bag filled with peppermint sticks, licorice strings, gumdrops, and chocolates.

Later on, the boat reached acres of vegetable farms. **8** 'What do you want today?' farmers called out. 'Lettuce, onions, and celery, please,' Mr. Garrity replied. After picking what was needed, the farmers tossed the

Lake Ontario

Lake Erie

CANADA

NEW YORK

Lockport

Tonawanda

Rochester

vegetables onto the slow-moving boat, and Mr. Garrity put coins into a raw potato and tossed it back. As the boat passed orchards farther along, Mr. Garrity sent Richard and James onshore to pick up the apples that had dropped to the ground. **9** He knew the boys were eager to help, but they were too young to work. Still, Richard dreamed about it. 'I'm going to be a hoggee and help Monkey Joe lead the mules,' he told James.

OVER AND UNDER

At Rochester, **10** Richard watched carefully as his father steered the boat and Monkey Joe guided the mules along the 802-foot aqueduct. Every time they crossed it, the children were amazed. Slowly and carefully, the *Sol Goldsmith* glided along a "highway of water" as the Erie Canal passed high above the Genesee River.

A while later Richard heard the call of the canal: "Low bridge. Everybody down!" 'Quick,' James said, and the two boys raced to the bow of the boat for their favorite trick. Because the boat rode high in the water—empty on its way home—the boys could jump up and grab on to the bottom of the bridge. Before their parents could stop them, they were

hanging from the bridge, laughing so hard they almost fell off. Just as the stern glided under the bridge, they dropped off onto the deck. **11**

ALMOST HOME

There was no playing around at Lockport. **12** Here the boat had to climb seventy feet up a rock wall. The mules strained to move the boat through one lock after another. At each level, gates closed behind and ahead of the boat. As water filled the lock, the boat rose to the next level. When the front gate opened, the mules towed the boat into the next, higher lock.

The next morning Richard was up early. He'd be glad to be home at Tonawanda **13** for a while. But Richard was a "canal boy" through and through. He couldn't wait to turn around and make another trip down the Erie Canal.

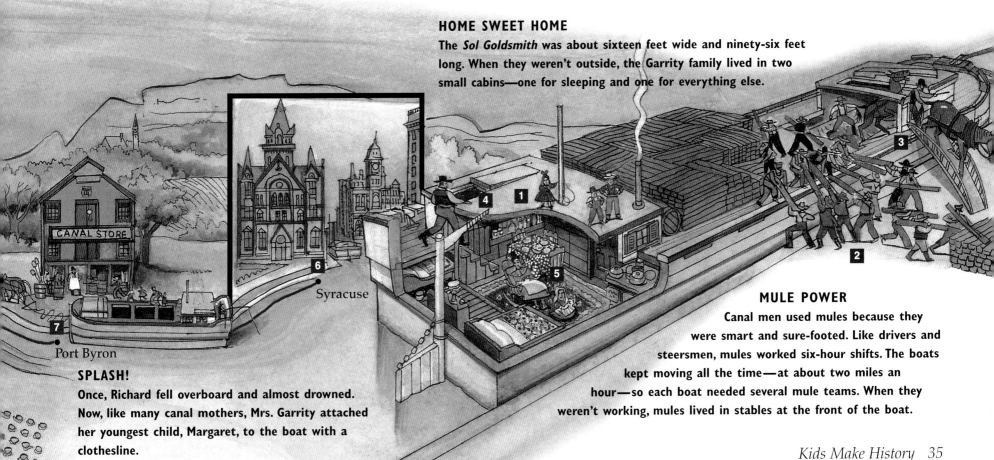

HOME SWEET HOME
The *Sol Goldsmith* was about sixteen feet wide and ninety-six feet long. When they weren't outside, the Garrity family lived in two small cabins—one for sleeping and one for everything else.

CANAL STORE

Syracuse

Port Byron

SPLASH!
Once, Richard fell overboard and almost drowned. Now, like many canal mothers, Mrs. Garrity attached her youngest child, Margaret, to the boat with a clothesline.

MULE POWER
Canal men used mules because they were smart and sure-footed. Like drivers and steersmen, mules worked six-hour shifts. The boats kept moving all the time—at about two miles an hour—so each boat needed several mule teams. When they weren't working, mules lived in stables at the front of the boat.

Riding the Orphan Train

1926

Watching the train come into the station, Al Clement held on to his younger brother Leo's hand. He wasn't sure where this train would take them, but he knew they needed to stay together. When their mother died two years earlier, the boys' father had taken them to the Jefferson County Orphan Asylum. **1** Nine-year-old Al knew that he and Leo weren't really orphans—orphans were children whose parents had both died. But Mr. Clement couldn't take care of his children, so he put Al and Leo in the orphanage.

Now Al, Leo, and ten other children from the orphanage were all dressed up, waiting to board this train. Suddenly Al heard a man call his name. Turning, he couldn't believe what he saw: his father, holding another brother, little Gerald. **2** For two years, Mr. Clement had never come to see Al and Leo. Now he handed them Gerald and a pink envelope. 'The train is taking you to find a family,' Mr. Clement said, 'a family who can care for you. When you are settled, send me this envelope so I'll know where you are.' As Al cried out that he didn't want a new family, adults pulled him away from his father. They led Al, Leo, and Gerald onto the "orphan train."

LOSING HOPE

As the train pulled out of the station, the matron in charge sternly ordered the boys to sit down. The orphan train was part of a plan to find new homes for children who had no families, she told them. Al had a different plan, though. Patting the pink envelope in his pocket, he thought about how he would find their father again.

At New York's Grand Central Station, **3** thirty-eight other orphans boarded the train. That night, while the children slept, the matron took the pink envelope from Al's pocket. 'You won't need that address any longer,' the matron told the horrified boy the next morning. Al thought his heart would break. Now he would never be able to find his father again.

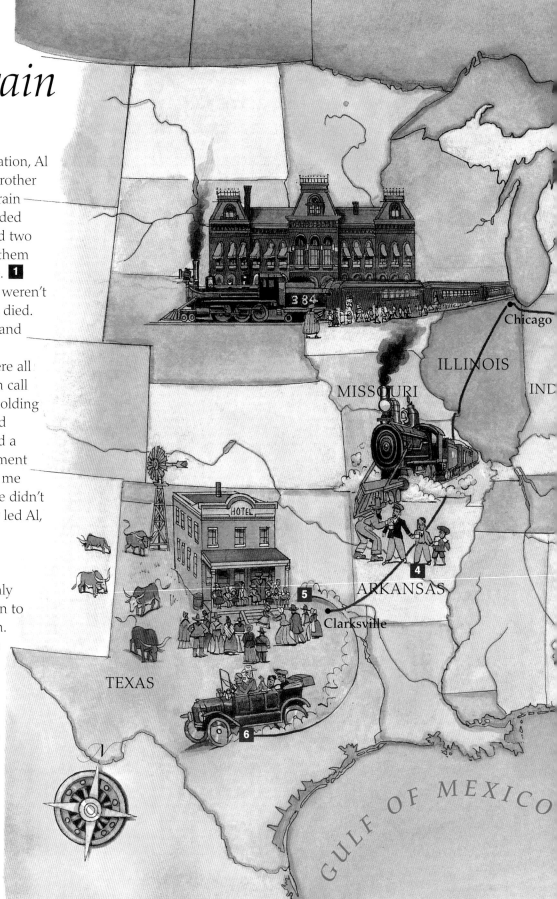

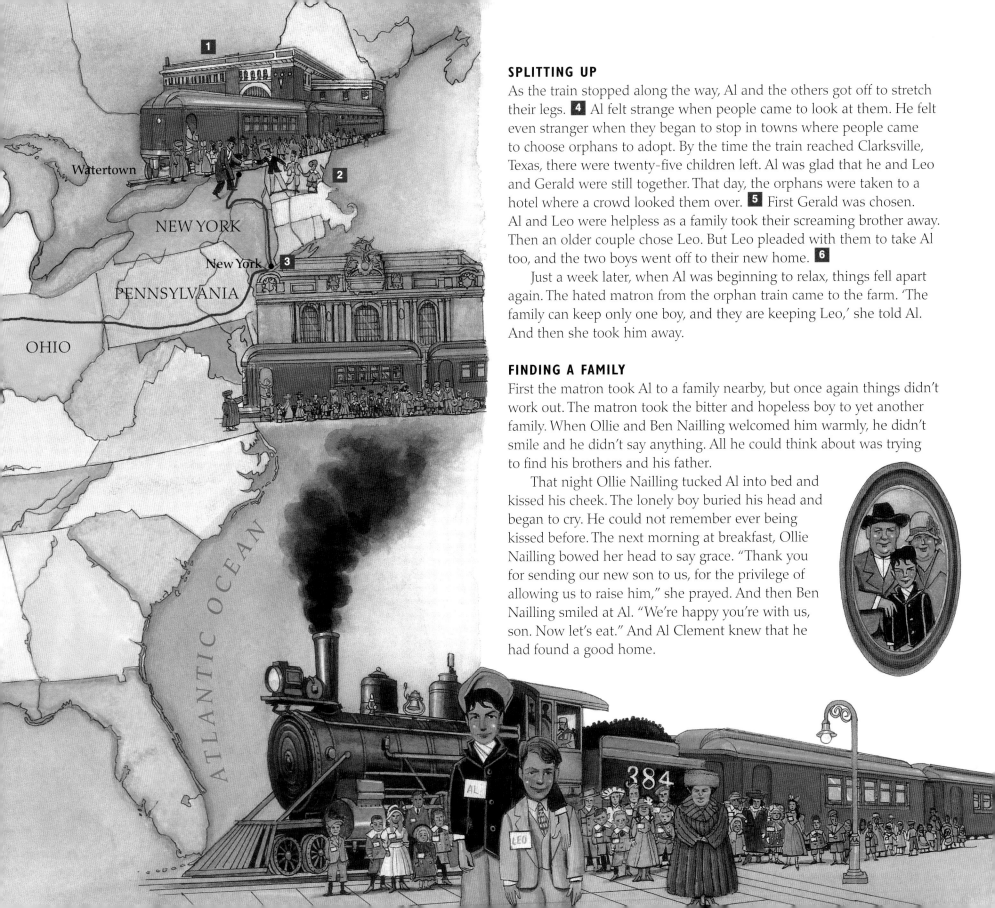

SPLITTING UP

As the train stopped along the way, Al and the others got off to stretch their legs. **4** Al felt strange when people came to look at them. He felt even stranger when they began to stop in towns where people came to choose orphans to adopt. By the time the train reached Clarksville, Texas, there were twenty-five children left. Al was glad that he and Leo and Gerald were still together. That day, the orphans were taken to a hotel where a crowd looked them over. **5** First Gerald was chosen. Al and Leo were helpless as a family took their screaming brother away. Then an older couple chose Leo. But Leo pleaded with them to take Al too, and the two boys went off to their new home. **6**

Just a week later, when Al was beginning to relax, things fell apart again. The hated matron from the orphan train came to the farm. 'The family can keep only one boy, and they are keeping Leo,' she told Al. And then she took him away.

FINDING A FAMILY

First the matron took Al to a family nearby, but once again things didn't work out. The matron took the bitter and hopeless boy to yet another family. When Ollie and Ben Nailling welcomed him warmly, he didn't smile and he didn't say anything. All he could think about was trying to find his brothers and his father.

That night Ollie Nailling tucked Al into bed and kissed his cheek. The lonely boy buried his head and began to cry. He could not remember ever being kissed before. The next morning at breakfast, Ollie Nailling bowed her head to say grace. "Thank you for sending our new son to us, for the privilege of allowing us to raise him," she prayed. And then Ben Nailling smiled at Al. "We're happy you're with us, son. Now let's eat." And Al Clement knew that he had found a good home.

Sunday Morning at Pearl Harbor

1941

Paradise—that's where Joan Zuber thought she was living. She loved everything about life on Ford Island in the middle of Hawaii's Pearl Harbor. For nine-year-old Joan and her sister, Peggy, Ford Island was a warm and flowery home—a place to play, to go to school, to learn Hawaiian songs and Hawaiian dances. Too soon, though, Joan Zuber would know that life was more complicated than hibiscus flowers and hula dancing. Too soon, she would understand the long-ago Hawaiian name for Ford Island: Mokuumeune, the Island of Strife.

LIVING ON BATTLESHIP ROW

The Zuber house sat across the lawn from Battleship Row. Every morning Joan woke to the bells that told time on the ships. She could even hear the music as the sailors did their morning exercises. Joan knew that those enormous battleships—the *Arizona, Maryland, Nevada, West Virginia, Tennessee,* and *Oklahoma*—were the reason that she was at Pearl Harbor. Her father, Major Adolph Zuber, was commander of the Marines stationed there. And she knew that her mother was frightened. "I feel war coming closer and closer," Alice Zuber told her husband. War had already spread across Europe. And in the Pacific, the powerful Japanese were a dangerous threat as they conquered one enemy after another.

THE SURPRISE ATTACK

On Sunday morning, December 7, war came to Pearl Harbor. A little before eight A.M., Joan curled up in a chair to read. Suddenly, gunfire boomed out. "A strange plane just flew right over my head!" she shouted as she found her parents. Then they saw the *West Virginia*. As the giant battleship tilted into the water, Major Zuber shouted, "My god . . . We're under bombardment! GET TO THE SHELTER!"

A NARROW ESCAPE

"Get your bathrobes . . . Carry your shoes!" Alice Zuber shouted as she led her daughters from the house. **1** Outside, bullets hit the ground as a Japanese plane flew overhead. "Get your heads down, bend over, and run as fast as you can!" Mrs. Zuber screamed. **2** At the Bachelor Officers Quarters, **3** men urged them inside. Outside, the *Arizona* exploded in "a rain of fire." **4** "Don't cry, Joan. Marines don't cry," Mrs. Zuber said. Joan thought of her father working to save his men, and she stopped weeping.

The flames of burning ships shot into the sky as a Marine drove the three Zubers to a safer spot, **5** away from Battleship Row. **6** For hours, women, children, and wounded men were crowded together in the shelter. When the "all clear" sirens sounded, the Zubers walked out into devastation: wounded men, wrecked planes, destroyed homes. The battleships "lay like shattered toys in a sea of burning oil," Joan thought. The broken body of a Japanese pilot had been dragged onto the lawn of the Zubers' home. Fearing another attack, Joan and Peggy spent the afternoon loading ammunition for machine guns. All around them was the sound of jack-hammers as people tried to rescue sailors imprisoned in the sunken ships. It was Wednesday before Joan saw her young father, who now looked "old and tired."

By Christmas, Joan and her mother and sister had left Pearl Harbor to return to the United States. Joan turned ten on the voyage, but there was no celebration. She felt "like a silent passenger in a strange world."

On the Circuit

1955

Carefully, proudly, Francisco read the story aloud to Mr. Lema, his sixth-grade teacher. As he said the English words correctly, Mr. Lema smiled and so did Francisco. For weeks, Mr. Lema had helped the eager boy every day at lunchtime. For Francisco Jiménez, there could have been no greater gift. More than anything in the world, Francisco wanted to go to school and learn to speak and read English as well as the Spanish he spoke at home and in the fields where he worked with his family.

That fall afternoon, Francisco could hardly wait to tell his parents about the day. But when he walked into their shack, his heart sank. All of the family's belongings were packed into cardboard boxes. Francisco realized that he would not see Mr. Lema again. Tomorrow, with his mother and father, his brothers and his little sister, he would leave for the next stop on "the circuit."

MOVING ON

Early the next morning Francisco and his older brother, Roberto, helped Papá and Mamá load their old car, Carcachita. They left Fresno, **1** where they'd been picking grapes for eight weeks, and moved on to the cotton fields near Corcoran, **2** stopping along the road to eat. Every year it was the same, Francisco thought sadly: a little school and then a lot of work. And picking cotton was a *lot* of work. Dragging a ten-foot sack, you filled it with cotton bolls until it weighed almost a hundred pounds. For that you were paid three cents a pound.

By the end of December, it was time to head back to Santa Maria **3** and the Bonetti Ranch. **4** The circuit always began and ended there. Francisco was glad to see people he knew, other migrant workers from Mexico like his own family. And he was happy because he would stay in one school until summer came.

ALMOST HOME

Life was not easy at the Bonetti Ranch. The wind blew in through holes in the walls of the rundown buildings. The water was undrinkable. And the house was invaded by fleas from stray dogs. For Francisco, though, it felt more like home than any other place on the circuit.

This year Francisco had a special project. Every day his teacher gave the class new words to define. Learning English words wasn't easy for Francisco, but he had a plan. At the city dump he'd found a small blue notepad. Francisco wrote down all of the new words in this little book, his *librito*. He studied them whenever he could.

After school and on weekends Francisco worked in the fields with Papá and Roberto. It was backbreaking work. In the lettuce fields, **5** you had to use a short hoe. Francisco complained, but he knew that the work was even harder for his father. Like other farm workers who had used the short hoe for years, Mr. Jiménez had terrible back trouble.

When summer came, the strawberries were ready for picking. **6** The work was hard, but Mr. Ito, the Japanese strawberry farmer, was so kind that Francisco didn't mind.

THE FIRE

In September the grapes were ready for picking in the San Joaquin Valley. All day long, Francisco worked in the fields near Orosi **7** with his father and two of his brothers. As he picked, he went over and over the words he had written in his little blue notebook.

One night, Mamá lit the fire in the kitchen of the old house where they were staying. Instantly, flames exploded in the kerosene stove. "*Salgan!* Get out!" Papá shouted. Outside, the family watched in horror as the house burned down. Papá managed to rescue the tin box that contained all of their savings, but Francisco's *librito* was gone. Mamá comforted the heartbroken boy. "If you know what was in your *librito*, then it's not all lost," she said.

LA MIGRA

By the time Francisco was in the eighth grade, everything had changed. With his bad back, Papá could no longer work, and the family decided to stay in Santa Maria. Francisco was afraid. How could he stay in school and also help the family? Then an even worse fear came true. One day *la Migra*—

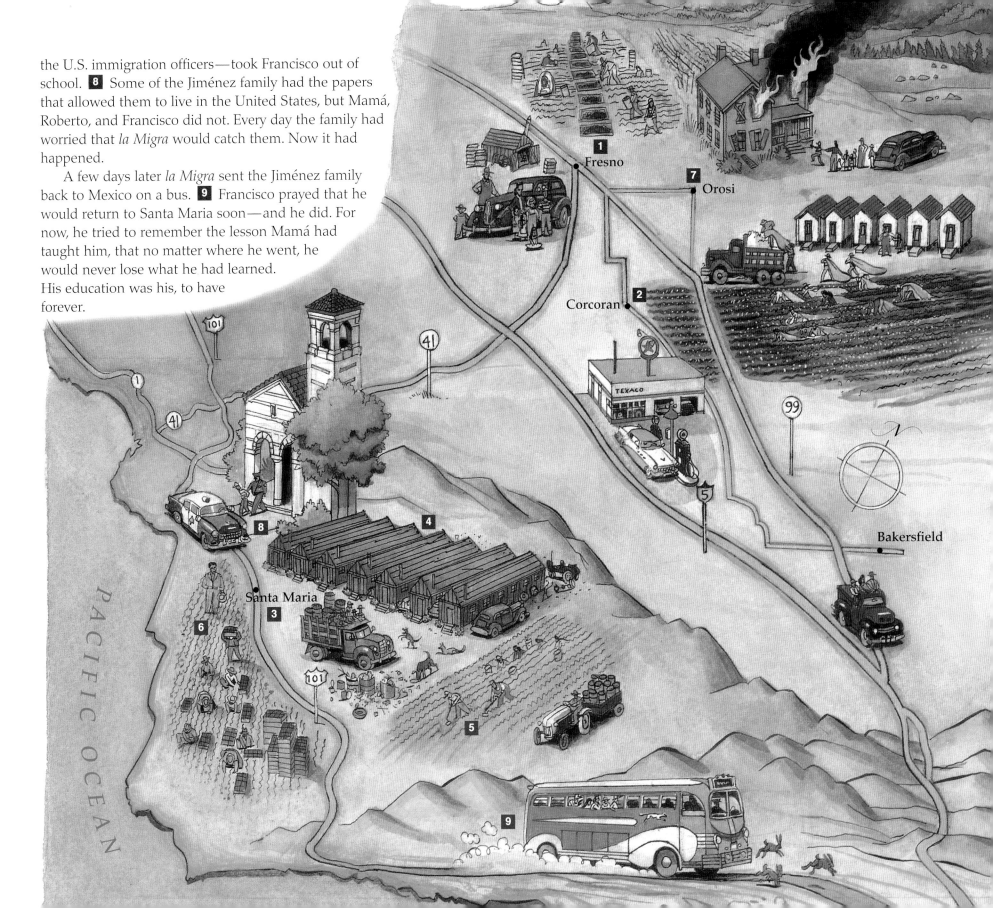

the U.S. immigration officers—took Francisco out of school. **8** Some of the Jiménez family had the papers that allowed them to live in the United States, but Mamá, Roberto, and Francisco did not. Every day the family had worried that *la Migra* would catch them. Now it had happened.

A few days later *la Migra* sent the Jiménez family back to Mexico on a bus. **9** Francisco prayed that he would return to Santa Maria soon—and he did. For now, he tried to remember the lesson Mamá had taught him, that no matter where he went, he would never lose what he had learned. His education was his, to have forever.

Fresno **1**

Orosi **7**

Corcoran **2**

TEXACO

Bakersfield

Santa Maria **3**

8

4

6

5

9

PACIFIC OCEAN

"It's About Freedom"

1963

Malcolm Hooks was going to be arrested. As he marched down the steps of Birmingham's Sixteenth Street Baptist Church,  the thirteen-year-old boy was ready. Boys and girls, mothers and fathers, all the marchers sang "We Shall Overcome" together. Malcolm's father took his son's hand and held it tightly.

Inside the church they had prayed, sung, and listened to the Reverend Fred Shuttlesworth and other civil rights leaders. "We're making history," Reverend Shuttlesworth had said as he sent the black children of Birmingham out to challenge the segregated world in which they lived. "You are fighting for what your country is and what it will be," he told them at the church.

Malcolm thought about what had brought him to this moment. He thought about what it was like to grow up African American in Alabama—sitting in the back of the bus and in the "colored section" at the movies. He thought about the names he'd been called and the things he hadn't been able to do because of the color of his skin. Malcolm rubbed the lucky ring he was wearing, his grandfather's ring, and he knew that his grandfather would have been proud of him today.

PROTESTS IN THE PARK

Malcolm could see what was happening in Kelly Ingram Park. **2** The park was full of black teenagers and even younger children, all protesting segregation. These protests were against city law, and officials were determined to stop them. Malcolm had seen the police dogs lunging at teenagers. **3** He had watched as firefighters turned hoses onto the crowds **4** and water shot out so hard that it stripped the bark off a tree and ripped the shirt right off a boy's back.

Now Malcolm had reached the bottom of the steps. Turning to look at his father, he knew what he was thinking: "I'm letting my son go and I know the danger, but we are compelled to do this. It's bigger than us." Mr. Hooks watched silently as Malcolm stepped into line. Two by two, still singing, the children turned toward downtown Birmingham. **5**

Along the way, Malcolm's brother, Earnest, came up to him. Looking worried, he tried to give Malcolm a knife for protection.

Malcolm refused, remembering all the lessons on nonviolence that he had learned from Fred Shuttlesworth and Martin Luther King, Jr.

ARRESTED DOWNTOWN

The streets downtown were filled with nonviolent protestors carrying signs, singing, and chanting. When an out-of-towner asked what this was all about, a teenager answered proudly. "It's about freedom," he said. Malcolm's group was headed for the "whites only" Holiday Inn. When they arrived, the teenagers went inside and sat quietly, as they'd been told to do. Right away the man at the desk shouted, "You can't sit here. Get out!" For five minutes, no one said a word.

Then the police arrived. Malcolm and the others were loaded into "paddy wagons" to go to jail. Still, Malcolm was not afraid—he was with friends, after all—but he was worried about his sister, Arnetta. She had marched with another group, and Malcolm didn't know what was happening to her.

For days, protesting Birmingham children—some as young as six years old—had been getting themselves arrested. Now the jail was so full that Malcolm was put into a cell with young men much older and rougher than he. Frightened, Malcolm slipped his precious ring onto a chain and dropped it underneath his clothes. He knew that he was in jail for doing something right, not something wrong, but now he was afraid. Then he rolled up his jacket for a pillow and tried to find a spot on the floor where he could sleep. Waiting for the lights to go out, he prayed. At about midnight, Malcolm heard his name called. Through a special window, he saw a beautiful sight: his parents had come to take him home.

MAKING A DIFFERENCE

The Hooks family talked over and over about what had happened. The children and their parents knew that there was more work ahead before "the old ways" would be changed. But they also knew that the black children of Birmingham had broken the back of segregation in their city. "I am hopeful," Malcolm said—"hopeful that I have done something to make a difference." And he had.

9/11: The Day the Towers Fell

2001

It was a beautiful September morning. In lower Manhattan, New Yorkers rushed to work past the gleaming towers of the World Trade Center. A few blocks away, in Stuyvesant High School, the first classes were ending. At 8:45 senior Jukay Hsu closed his books and thought about what he had to do that Tuesday as president of the student union. At 8:46 the day exploded.

THE PLANES HIT

In his classroom on the north side of Stuyvesant, Jukay felt the floor shake. Within minutes, sirens screamed up the West Side Highway ten floors below. The loudspeaker crackled as principal Stanley Teitel announced, "A plane has hit the north tower of the World Trade Center." **1** Was this some small plane that had lost its way? students wondered. On the south side of Stuyvesant, however, Jukay's friend Amit Friedlander could see the World Trade Center. He watched in horror as bodies fell from the flaming north tower.

At 9:03 a second plane hit the south tower. **2** On the television in his classroom, **3** Jukay saw a fireball envelop the south tower. Now he knew that this was no accident.

EXIT THE BUILDING

Everywhere, students were trying to call home on their cell phones, but there was no service. "Why are we still here when something terrible is happening?" Jukay wondered. "Won't the towers fall on us?" Stanley Teitel had the same worry. With no phone or computer service, the school was cut off from the outside world. Then FBI and Secret Service agents arrived to set up a command center at the school. 'There is no chance of the towers falling,' they told the principal. But just before 10:00, in a shattering roar, the south tower of the World Trade Center collapsed. Fearing that shock waves could bring down their building too, the administration decided to evacuate the school immediately.

When the announcement came, Jukay rushed downstairs 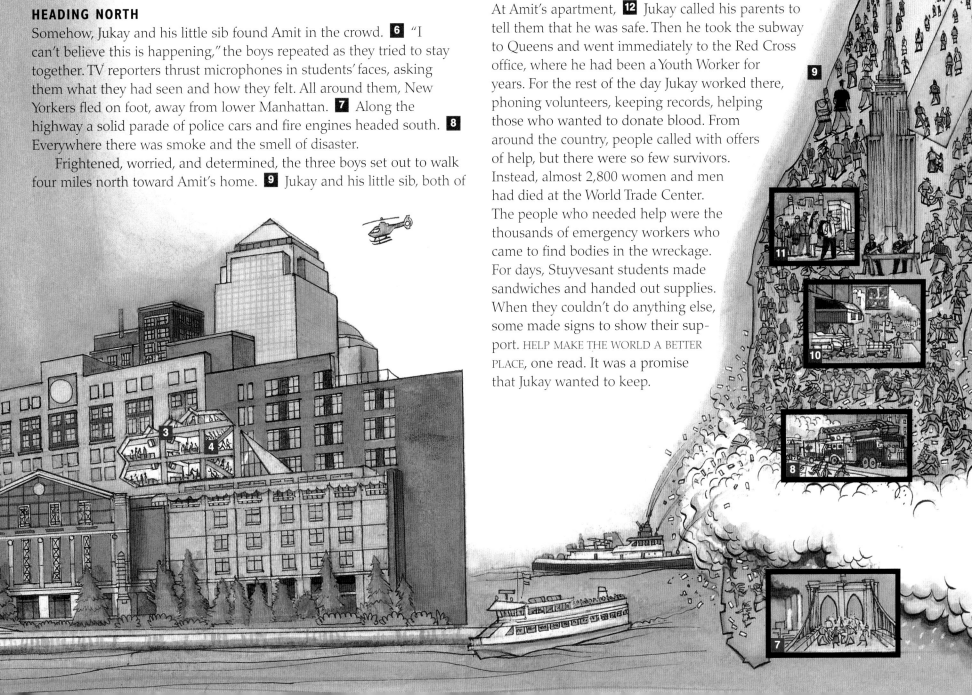**4** to find his "little sib," the freshman boy he mentored. Everywhere, frightened students searched for their friends and tried to remain calm. At the school's north doors, the assistant principal stood on a chair. "Keep moving slowly, exit the building, and move north. Just keep moving north," he called out as the three thousand students left, two hundred at a time. **5**

HEADING NORTH

Somehow, Jukay and his little sib found Amit in the crowd. **6** "I can't believe this is happening," the boys repeated as they tried to stay together. TV reporters thrust microphones in students' faces, asking them what they had seen and how they felt. All around them, New Yorkers fled on foot, away from lower Manhattan. **7** Along the highway a solid parade of police cars and fire engines headed south. **8** Everywhere there was smoke and the smell of disaster.

Frightened, worried, and determined, the three boys set out to walk four miles north toward Amit's home. **9** Jukay and his little sib, both of whom lived across the East River in Queens, had no idea how or when they could go home. As they walked north, another massive cloud of smoke and debris billowed up when the second tower collapsed behind them. At hospitals, doctors waited for the survivors who would never come. **10** People everywhere were trying to call their loved ones. **11**

TRYING TO HELP

At Amit's apartment, **12** Jukay called his parents to tell them that he was safe. Then he took the subway to Queens and went immediately to the Red Cross office, where he had been a Youth Worker for years. For the rest of the day Jukay worked there, phoning volunteers, keeping records, helping those who wanted to donate blood. From around the country, people called with offers of help, but there were so few survivors. Instead, almost 2,800 women and men had died at the World Trade Center. The people who needed help were the thousands of emergency workers who came to find bodies in the wreckage. For days, Stuyvesant students made sandwiches and handed out supplies. When they couldn't do anything else, some made signs to show their support. HELP MAKE THE WORLD A BETTER PLACE, one read. It was a promise that Jukay wanted to keep.

Acknowledgments

Once again we have had the privilege of partnership—authors, illustrator, designer, editors. Like its predecessors *Journeys in Time* and *Places in Time,* this book could not have been created without that collaboration.

Artist Randy Jones was as imaginative, funny, and wonderful this time as he was before. With immense talent—and the invaluable partnership of his wife, Susann Ferris Jones—Randy invites all of us into the worlds that he creates on paper. We thank him for being our partner and our friend.

Designer Kevin Ullrich made our ideas work on the page. His talent and friendship—and patience!—were invaluable now as before.

Our first editor, Amy Flynn, made this series happen in the beginning, and we thank her for her faith in us and in our dream. Emily Linsay was a gift for which we will be eternally grateful. And Eleni Beja has guided us to the end of this journey with marvelous care and skill.

As before, we have relied on the expertise and generosity of historians, librarians, archivists, and curators around the country. In addition to those listed here, we continue to be grateful to the generations of historians whose wisdom we have tapped and to the libraries where we found it (especially to the Bobst Library at New York University, the New York Public Library, and the New York Society Library).

Susan Buckley
Elspeth Leacock

Notes

Every story and every person in this book is real. We met these "kids" in many places—we read about them in books, we talked with historians, and sometimes we were lucky enough to interview the subjects themselves.

Sometimes we know exactly what people said. Then we have used regular quotation marks for dialogue. In other cases, we have a good idea about what people said but we do not have solid historical evidence. For this dialogue we have used single quotation marks.

Powhatan's Favorite Daughter

In reconstructing a *true* story of Pocahontas, we relied primarily on the inestimable advice of Helen C. Rountree, professor emerita of anthropology at Old Dominion University in Virginia. Dr. Rountree, esteemed as the world's leading expert on the Powhatan Indians, is the author of many scholarly works as well as a book for younger readers, *Young Pocahontas in the Indian World* (Virginia Publications, 1995). Thanks to Helen Rountree; Nancy Egloff, historian, Jamestown-Yorktown Foundation; Diane Stallings; and Ted Wolf.

James Towne Boy

Samuel Collier was one of the four boys who came to Virginia in 1607. Like other information about the early days of the settlement, facts about Sam are scanty and sometimes contradictory. With the help of scholars like Nancy Egloff, we have constructed a story that we believe to be true. Some of our information comes from the writings of John Smith, including the description of Pocahontas' bringing the gifts from her father. We relied on the excellent works of archaeologist and historian

Ivor Noel Hume for theories on the start of the fire, as well as other aspects of the story. Gail Karwoski told Sam's story in her book *Surviving Jamestown* (Peachtree Publishers, 2001). Thanks to Nancy Egloff, historian, Jamestown-Yorktown Foundation.

Evil in the Air

Much of what we know about the goings-on in Salem comes from the detailed transcripts kept of all of the interrogations and trials. Quoted material is taken from those transcripts. Thanks to Mary Beth Norton, professor of American history at Cornell University and her book *In the Devil's Snare* (Alfred A. Knopf, 2002); Marc Aronson, author of *Witch-Hunt* (Atheneum, 2003); and archivist Richard Trask at the Peabody Institute Library, Danvers, Massachusetts.

Kidnapped

After years of searching for a sufficiently detailed story of an indentured servant, we found a description of Peter Williamson's adventures in Steven Mintz's book *Huck's Raft* (Belknap/Harvard, 2004). Peter tells his own remarkable tale, said to be the basis for Robert Louis Stevenson's *Kidnapped,* in his book *The Curious Adventures of Peter Williamson Who Was Kidnapped at Aberdeen and Sold for a Slave in America.* (We found the thirtieth edition of that book, printed in 1865, at the New York Public Library.) Thanks to John Van Der Zee, Patricia Dennison, and Gordon DesBrisay.

Yankee Doodle Soldier

Joseph Plumb Martin told his own story in *A Narrative of Some of the Adventures, Dangers, and Sufferings of a Revolutionary Soldier.* Thanks to Robert Grumet for his invaluable help and introductions; Robert M. S. McDonald, assistant professor of history, U. S. Military Academy, West Point; and Gary Wheeler Stone, Resource Interpretive Specialist, Historic Resources, Monmouth Battlefield State Park.

The House on the Hill

In addition to the original accounts by members of the Rankin family, our most important source for this story was the exhaustive research of author Ann Hagedorn in writing *Beyond the River* (Simon & Schuster, 2002), her book on Ripley, Ohio, and the Underground Railroad. Hagedorn used letters, court records, diaries, weather reports, and her own knowledge of the locale to reconstruct the story of Eliza and Chancey Shaw. "It represents a very very important part of the history of the Underground Railroad," she told us. "It shows what people will do to gain their freedom . . . and in the character of Shaw, it shows that witnessing slavery or an escape can convert even an alleged criminal." Thanks to Ann Hagedorn; Alison Gibson, Union Township Public Library, Ripley, Ohio; and Carol Lloyd, Underground Railroad Freedom Center, Cincinnati, Ohio.

"Never Take No Cutoffs"

The name "Donner Party" immediately brings to mind the horrors of cannibalism, of course. We decided not to bring cannibalism into this story of the Reed family for two reasons: first, the Reeds managed not to consume any of their fellow travelers, and second, it would have been impossible to deal with this subject sensitively or honestly in such a compressed story. Thanks to California author Jim Houston.

Pony Rider

Elijah Nicholas Wilson (Nick Wilson) told his story in *The White Indian Boy: The Story of Uncle Nick Among the Shoshones* (Fredonia Books, 2001).

Pull-Up Boy

Marty Myers is one of the people brought back to life in the remarkable exhibits at Pittsburgh's Heinz History Center. Thanks to Ann Fortescue, David Grinnell, Anne Madarasz, Hilary Palevsky of the Senator John Heinz Pittsburgh Regional History Center, and Charles McCollester.

Working for Freedom

Susie Baker King Taylor told her story in *A Black Woman's Civil War Memoirs: Reminiscences of My Life in Camp with the 33rd U.S. Colored Troops, Late 1st South Carolina Volunteers* (Markus Wiener Publishers, 1988).

Pioneer Girl

Along with recent biographies, Laura Ingalls Wilder's much-loved books provide a rich guide to the story of her life. Thanks to Vivian Glover, Laura Ingalls Wilder Memorial Society, DeSmet, South Dakota.

"There Blows!"

George Fred told his own story in *"Cap'n George Fred" Himself* (Doubleday, 1928). Our story is based on this account. The actual ship's log describes a slightly more complicated journey. Thanks to Laura Pereira at the New Bedford Whaling Museum, New Bedford, Massachusetts.

"A Most Wonderful Sight"

In the collection of Chicago's Newberry Library are four letters that Jane Sever wrote to her family at home. All quoted material comes from those letters. Thanks to Martha Briggs, associate curator of modern manuscripts, Roger and Julie Baskes Department of Special Collections, Newberry Library, Chicago, Illinois.

High Jinks in the White House

In addition to the many anecdotes on the Roosevelt children recounted in biographies of Theodore Roosevelt and the memoirs of Alice Roosevelt Longworth, we found acounts in the memoir *Forty-Two Years in the White House* by Irwin Hood Hoover (Houghton Mifflin, 1934). Thanks to historian John Riley, director of education and scholarship programs, White House Historical Association.

Low Bridge!

Richard Garrity told his own story in *Canal Boatman: My Life on Upstate Waterways* (Syracuse University Press, 1979). Thanks to Andrew Kitzmann, historian, Erie Canal Museum, Syracuse, New York.

Riding the Orphan Train

We first read Al Nailling's story in Andrea Warren's *Orphan Train Rider: One Boy's True Story* (Houghton Mifflin, 1996), a book based on interviews with Mr. Nailling. Al Nailling (renamed Lee when he was adopted) was able to remain in close contact with his brothers, but none of them ever saw their father again. Al was raised by his adoptive parents, Ben and Ollie Nailling. Thanks to Andrea Warren.

Sunday Morning at Pearl Harbor

Joan Zuber Earle told her own dramatic story in *The Children of Battleship Row* (RDR Books, 2002). Thanks to Joan Zuber Earle.

On the Circuit

Francisco Jiménez generously shared his story with us in interviews, as well as in his two books *The Circuit* (Houghton Mifflin, 1997) and *Breaking Away* (Houghton Mifflin, 2001). Thanks to Francisco Jiménez.

"It's About Freedom"

Malcolm Hooks told us his story in fascinating conversations, as well as in the oral history recorded at the Birmingham Civil Rights Institute. Thanks to Malcolm Hooks; Mrs. Jimmie Hooks; and Dr. Horace Huntley and Laura Anderson, Birmingham Civil Rights Institute, Birmingham, Alabama.

9/11: The Day the Towers Fell

Jukay Hsu and Amit Friedlander bravely relived their stories for us in interviews. We also spoke with other Stuyvesant students and faculty who were there that day. The Fall 2001 special edition of the *Spectator*, the Stuyvesant newspaper, provided important information, as well. Thanks to Jukay Hsu, Amit Friedlander, Zoe Ellis, Elka Gould, and Renee Levine.

Index